I0159827

IF TRUTH
WERE TO BE TOLD

SAKET SURYESH

Serene Woods
www.serenewoods.com

Text copyright © Saket Suryesh 2010
Cover photo copyright © HAMI 2010

This book is sold subject to the condition that it shall not, by way of trade or otherwise, be lent, resold, hired out, or otherwise circulated without Serene Woods' prior written consent in any form of binding or cover other than that in which it is published and without a similar condition including this condition being imposed on the subsequent purchaser and without limiting the rights under copyright reserved above, no part of this publication maybe reproduced, stored in or introduced into a retrieval system or transmitted in any form or by any means (electronic, mechanical, photocopying, recording or otherwise) without the permission of both the copyright owner and Serene Woods.

ISBN: 978-93-80112-18-3

Printing and Binding: Thomson Press (India) Limited

Cover Design: Hami (www.facebook.com/getyourhami)

To

**Sanskriti,
my daughter,
my soul and my salvation...**

Introduction

As I write, I get better. With words, I am able to comprehend the world around me better. My thoughts flow into words, as if being automatically written on paper. Long ago, I used to write. I was certainly a better person. Even with little money, love and worldly possessions, I was happier, searching and yet at peace with myself, for I could, all the time write and try to make sense of the world around me, joining incoherent dots to make coherent pictures. Somewhere, in my journey to become something, I betrayed myself and what I was supposed to become. This incoherence, led to an internal destruction and a lack of courage to face the man in the mirror.

A difficult phase of ill health and several difficult years of growing up or rather, growing down, left me a shadow, a poor caricature of what I was and what I was capable of becoming. Even when I received a blessing, a beautiful daughter, my pain just kept flowing. It left marks like those left on a smoother road by a vehicle suddenly brought to a screeching halt. As I was juggled around by my various relationships, each seemed to be pulling me in a different direction. In the end, I felt untrue to all of them and above all, to myself. It drained me to such an extent that writing, which was my second nature, became a scary thought. I was scared of what might come out on paper. I thought of my words staring back at me. Would it be painful, embarrassing?

Sometimes, it felt I could write no more; the words would float before my eyes and as I would try to catch hold of them, they would slip off like fish in the water. I could not take it anymore - this feeling of numbness, of being nothing and of the constant state of stupefaction. So, what I write here is not much of an attempt at pedagogy, but my attempt at teaching myself to live this mystery called life. I am no Guru and my experiences in life would invariably be no different from the reader of this book. This is my attempt to understand the world around me and to understand my own place in the ecosystem of different entities and their inter-relationship and their relationship with me. As I stand on the fence, I decide not to let life pass by me and to take on the challenges thrown at me by the tides of time.

As I stand on the shoulders of the giants – the Nietzsches, the Ayn Rands and the others, sometimes I find myself contradicting them, since I believe that a pupil who is not able to contradict his teachers, insults their teachings. I learn from them to gain a vantage point, a peak from where I jump into the realm of the unknown, to explore the world around me, to try to make sense out of what surrounds me and what is within me.

This book is my attempt to get better, with greater understanding and clarity of purpose. In the age of too much information and little knowledge, where interpersonal skills are judged by the number of social networking sites you use, where grief is shared on twitter, hand-holding has lost relevance, relationships are taken as a direct derivative of usefulness, this book attempts to re-kindle the fire which Prometheus once brought to the Earth, the light which separates human beings from the other species. Through this book, I have been able to celebrate the nights which were lonelier than I thought I would ever face and the pain, which was deeper than I thought I would ever come across and even the happiness, which was more hysterical than I thought I would experience.

This book comes with all my love for my lovely daughter, Sanskriti who has brought me alive to the promise that life held for me, for my wife, Seema, who always stood by me and for my parents, who did their best to endow me with the ability to not only live, but to also try to understand the whys and wherefores of life, in order to live better and to keep on growing as I learn, every single day of my life, every single moment of my life. I thank my parents. I am gratified for my past, for it gave me my experiences and the insight to make sense of it. My wife, I thank for my present. The present makes me bold enough to write. My daughter, I thank for my future. I leave this document as a testament to my love for her and as a gift which will help her understand her own life better. I must also thank my friends for their support, appreciation and encouragement.

Going With the Flow

"This is Love: to fly towards a secret Sky, to cause a hundred Veils to fall each moment. First, to let go of life and finally, to take a step without feet."

- Jalal-Ud-Din Rumi

The joy of freefall is one of the earliest pleasures of life that a child experiences. Only later in life when we feel secure in the knowledge that the hand which threw us up is there to hold us on the way back do we come to note the feel of the nostalgic wind, the intoxication that comes with rising up each day that kept thrilling the child till the time he has to face the first fall of his life.

Possibly it continues even further, may be till the time the memory is not strong enough to remember the fall for a long time. And once we can remember well enough, a worry, a scare seeps in, which makes it so difficult to let go. Even if not all people end up being acrophobic, still it becomes so difficult to even remotely recall the feeling of euphoria associated with freefall.

How, then would you build your house on the slopes of Vesuvius, as Nietzsche advocated, with these fears lurking somewhere deep within your psyche? On deeper analysis, we find that it is not that we feel we are going to hit the ground and we fear the impact, but it is the fear of the unknown, the fear of not knowing when exactly we are going to hear the thud, as we touch the ground. As we grow up in life, we get into the tendency of calculating and pre-calculating the paths that we choose, trying to predict every bend, every turn of the path ahead of us. This is what causes us a great deal of stress and at times, even leads to an eventual state of non-action.

Yet, it would be wrong to completely negate and contradict all the wise sayings about not only planning ahead, but also writing down the plans, in order to be able to achieve what you want to achieve; Yes, it is true that you do need to know where you are going, but that means just the destination. You do not actually need to know each and every turn you are going to take and each random location where you are going to pause to catch a breath. You do not need to pre-calculate every turn and then get so tied up at each of the 'planned' milestones that there is no pleasure of exploration left, even when assuming that you are finally able to connect all the dots and are led to the final destination and assuming that you are motivated enough by choice or necessity to embark on the pre-planned path, at the chosen moment. The sad part is that at each milestone, at each of these dots, you will either reach too early or too late, or the dots will not be found to be exactly at the pre-ordained place and so, at every such point, you will end up asking yourself if you must, in spite of these variances from the original plan continue moving or consider, each such deviation as your own failure, causing your own disbelief, thereby abandoning the journey itself. I am not hereby, urging you to jump off the cliffs (or roof tops), but rather to have a destination and a direction, and then move on without sitting at a place and planning each step, each movement and each thought that you intend to have with each movement.

Suppose you wish to be friends with someone. You start to recall all the Carnegie ideas, erect your posture, get prepared to look into the eyes of the person in question, enacting and rehearsing the scene in your mind as you keep on playing it back and forth. Unfortunately, the person in question does not understand the imagined friendly posture. Obviously, he or she is not aware of the mental exercise that you are doing, oblivious to your meticulous planning; the person leaves. You are left there, out in the cold, all stressed out. Would it not be wonderful to just go out because you wish to speak to a person, even if you make a fool out of yourself, in the worst case scenario? Is it not better to have loved and lost, than to have never loved at all? Don't worry whether the cart comes before the horse or vice-versa, as long as the damn thing moves!

A leaving train will cause stress only if you are trying to catch it - a simple statement, with profound truth. What you intend to do is to reach a place, not that you reach by a particular train or a particular bus. What is important? The train? The bus? Or the destination? You miss a train. Catch another. Find yourself free for five hours? Have a good time at the platform, read something, bless your soul, for this slip gives you a time to just 'stand and stare'. Just ask yourself when was the last time you looked at the new, green twig on the tree, or the droplets of rain, slowly forming shapes and falling from the iron railing. Just think of the immense peace that you feel out of just thinking of it, and then try to relearn how to do it again in today's time and age.

One would argue that reaching a destination at a given point of time is what is more important, where time is the function of the value which is attached to the arrival at a point. Then, where does missing the train leave someone? Now, look at the significance we assign to this activity, calling it a matter of life or death. Having missed the train and still being alive, are we not prompted to reconsider the significance that we had earlier assigned to the act? Our being alive proves that it is not life or death at stake. Anything less than that is not worth losing our sleep over and losing our sanity over. Anything equal to that will again not matter in the end (you won't be alive to fret over it).

It is important to have a clear perspective of the destination. It is amazing to note how we spend a large part of our life sleepwalking. We keep on doing things, believing that we understand what we are intending to get out of our doings, while for the most part, we do not know what we are trying to aim for. The two most essential drivers for the entire life force are self-preservation and happiness. Anything other than those is just an aberration, a mere lack of clarity and understanding.

Take another case. We want to go to a place not to just attend a marriage, but ultimately to attend a marriage so that we can bless the couple, wishing them happiness. Some may counter argue that many events are attended not out of happiness but out of social necessity. Fine. We get ourselves a flight booked to reach the place, but then do we refuse to be treated with refreshments onboard, or do we switch off the air conditioning, even when we are feeling hot, just because feeling pleasure on the way was not the main idea or plan? By the same logic, one, there is nothing called social necessity. You are doing it because you feel a belongingness towards the social circle and you feel that gaining respect by attending a social function, which otherwise you are not keen on, will make you happy. So the argument rests here, you are going through an unpleasant exercise because in the end you want to be happy. Then, just think deeply, can't you be happy en route as well? There is a possibility that with this in mind, you may be able to shift your goal (of being happy) earlier, to the act of attending the social occasion itself. Then, possibly during the event you will be doing things which would be unexpected of you, at least initially. You might think, you will make an ass of yourself (if I may use the term) but I would say, doing so, attempting to be happy during the process of reaching where you want to go, you will be making human of yourself, and having done that, you will realize, you do not care to go any further, about making it to the social circle, because the happiness that it will offer, has already been attained by you, in the journey to that point itself. Enjoy the journey as much as the destination is what I urge you to do.

I would always start for work at my regular time and would assume to reach my workplace at the routine time, which is a reasonable expectation, to make an estimate. However, the entire dynamic ecosystem which will eventually comprise the journey might have a different plan. I end up twenty minutes late and at each point of traffic snarl was cursing, fuming and honking. Does it help? No, am I able to reach significantly earlier than I would have if I had just sat there silently, may be enjoying the music, enjoying the view (there of course, is some symmetry in the way cars line up and some joy in experiencing life manifesting itself in multiple forms around you - people chatting in the next car, a baby looking out of the car window, kids in the school bus)? No. Would it have significantly improved things for me had I reached earlier? I guess not. Am I terribly hurt or lost or failed for being delayed by ten minutes? I am sure not. The stress and the fume was not due to any other reason, but simply because I had mentally so seriously rehearsed my entire drive that any deviation is like missing the train I wanted to catch, thereby inducing stress. My concern should have been the destination, which was my workplace and why I was going to go there, which was to meet people of different hues, adding colors to my life, because I was going to put my brains to analyze a few things, putting it to exercise, thus pushing away possibilities of Alzheimer's, because I wanted to create something, to be put to use and to scream out in happiness for the simple state of being alive - so happy that tears would flow from the corner of the eye.

I, therefore, urge you to pick a destination and pick a direction. Clearing an exam could be your destination and studying for it, the direction. No planning beyond this is necessary and it is only going to be counterproductive. Even so close to our times, Donald Rumsfield, US Secretary of Defense said, "Do not over-control like novice pilot. Stay loose enough from the flow that you can observe it, modify and improve it."

Best things in life are not planned; best ideas are not conceived on the hill-top, but come out of the grind that we call life. When, what we call life is allowed to touch our souls so deep that we come out completely drenched in it, filled by fun, happiness and sometimes, even by sorrow, all great creations comes out of this ability to will for the destination and the direction and the willingness to let yourself flow with it. As Emerson says, "Finish each day and be done with it. You have done what you could...Tomorrow is a new day, you shall begin it well and serenely."

*****

Being Unique

"Every man has his own courage, and is betrayed because he seeks in himself the courage of other persons"

- *Ralph Waldo Emerson*

I have seen the pain. I have been through despair, which was brought about by the feeling of being left alone in the cold and damp corner of the horizon of your thoughts. I sure, would have survived your anger and disgust but what is killing me is the indifference. All of life's exercise is a struggle to be loved, initially the love of parents, which, one is certain of till the time you outgrow it, then it is a lookout for the love of friends and society, sometimes camouflaged as sympathy, empathy and sometime as respect or acceptance.

Every individual is born with some unique dreams and ideas. In fact, apart from the biologically defined body form, which can be possibly categorized by types, it is these ideas and dreams that bring unique hues and colours to the persona. They create a persona which echoes the great creativity of a nature that works incessantly to create individuals in a manner by which they are supposed to be and are, in truth, uniquely different from others. Dr. Wayne Dyer said, "Self-actualized people are independent of other people's opinion." I want to turn it around and add that becoming independent of other people's opinion leads to self-actualization. Accept that you are different from the person next door and then rather than working on being the same as others, cultivate your points of differentiation. Be more of what you are.

It is the want of approval and the want of love that forces one to kill the dreams, to change the stripes, to fit into the realm of acceptability. It is so painful to see the process by which each of the coloured feathers is taken off so that we end up bland and indistinct. The end of the process is twice as painful as the process itself; when you lie in a pool of blood drawn out of your own dead dreams, and worse, you cannot even smell the dead which surrounds you and start moving around dressed in blood covered clothes with a nonchalance of 'So what?'

The surrounding world claps furiously, as you step forward to join the group in which everyone is alike; the creativity of the Creator, thus defeated, only can watch you helplessly going forward to join the herd. Your wit is limited to the extent of silly smiles on account of someone's shape of nose. Your wisdom is limited to the extent of the ability to shortchange people (without even realizing that in the end it is you, who is being terribly shortchanged by life itself). While earlier you used to have fun with minimal accessories (a tea stall with broken bench would have done), now you invite people, sometimes lure them to come with you, looking for the best ambience, the best food and then you go through a hollow affair, waiting for the whole ordeal to be over so that you can retire to your own corner.

My old friends would come to me and find someone they could not recognize anymore and I could not recognize them anymore. We seemed to have walked a long distance away from each other. They would come, in anticipation of meeting someone who was so different from every other person they knew, and then they seemed shocked by the lack of shock, for I am much like any other person they would have known. Their disappointment is so telling that I am embarrassed to the sole of my foot, for not having lived up to what was expected of me, for not having realized the potential that I had held within my being. And then, I try to make up for it by external things - a wine pricier, a place costlier and still at the end of the meet, we depart, terribly feeling short-changed.

There is a fallacy, which pronounces 'All men are equal'. The truth is that by agreeing to this, we are insulting the creativity of the big Creator, of nature; we are implying the lack of innovativeness, lack of ingenuity in Nature's own design. Men are not equal, nor are they supposed to be. Men are supposed to be unequal, different. That is what brings beauty and adventure to life. To be more specific, perhaps men ought to be treated as equal but men are not identical and therefore, they must not be treated in an identical fashion. Some men would certainly deserve more civility while some would deserve more hostility. Treating the two alike will only disappoint both the ends and will only show a lack of wisdom on your part.

It is very important to pay heed to the man within you, who tells you to be silent or to speak, and so shall you behave. If a man with a serious temperament tries to be funny, he looks like he has lost his marbles, while a man who is instinctively funny, if he tries to be serious, will come across as an impersonator. Not only would it leave the audience wanting, he himself would be left feeling robbed of some significant part of his persona. The utter failure and destruction would be when he would even stop noticing the lack in his totality, on account of the desire to fit in and the desire to be loved by all. And once he loses it, even those whose love he had longed for would not recognize him anymore and would leave him.

I therefore, urge you to look deep inside yourself, to seek, to identify and to recognize yourself; and having done that, to move all heaven and earth to regain the lost you. Try to find the friend that you used to come across on the other side of the mirror every day, the one who knew you so well and the one you knew so well, with whom you never felt lonely in the most solitary of the cold nights. Do not try to exercise the muscles you never had. Do not try to expand the faculty you have never been blessed with. Find what you have. Find what is given to you. Build like crazy upon it, for time is fleeting and we are insignificant souls on a very small planet of a very ordinary star, in the immenseness of space and time. Do not try to be what you are not. Try to be more of what you are, so that you shine with the splendor of a thousand stars, whatever may be the duration. In a limitless sea of time 'how long' measured on a human scale does not matter. 'How deep' is what really matters.

Paint the pictures waiting to be painted. Play the music that is silently flowing in your blood. Write the book that is to be written, NOW! If you write it now, ten years hence, you will be able to improvise and get better and write another one, paint another one, play another one. You owe it to the One who bestowed upon you those unique faculties. You will then be loved more, even, when you are busy dancing at the edge of life.

*****

Standing with One Another

*"The true triumph of reason is that it enables us
to get along with those who do not possess it"*

- *Voltaire*

In today's professional world or otherwise in life, you just need to look a little deeper and you see the significance of networking. It is not something that is gaining currency now, in the world of globalization as the rightists would say, or westernization as leftists would say. It is something that has been around probably since the time man came out of the cave to live in a society where one person interacted with the other. The way one person lived and behaved was largely impacted by the people around him or the society that he lived in.

Unlike non thinking animals, the thinking man derives his power from the power he has over men who he calls his circle. The caveman who ruled the group was the one voted to rule, partly due to his capability and partly because of the number of people on whom he held sway. Man, with his individual stature and strength could not have survived a day in the forest, with more powerful animals roaming around. What kept him alive was the strength in numbers. The more the number, the more was the strength. Call it any name; there was always democracy. It was the power of the people that made kings wise or mad. It did not come from the physical or military strength that one held. Many a sages, with little to speak of their own physical or martial power, held more power than the kings simply because they had big kings (again, big by number of people in their army) over whom they held sway. The long and short of it is that networking has historic origins. It has grown into an art through years of refinement.

It is not a tool for the lowly people; it is a necessity for the able ones. Able people, simply by virtue of their ability, make themselves indispensable. Through their hard work and dedication, they become more able and hence, less and less tolerant of mediocrity, which in turn, teams up in having beer together and amorally laughing together in relationships with no depth, but with plenty of calculation. A lone man with capability is like a deer out in the front of a pride of lions. He has no protection, no support or backup. Sometimes, he tries to fit in, in the same group of mediocrity, in spite of feeling the shallowness of the relationships there. He is like a man on the top of the cliff, taking a plunge into the large expanse of water, only to find that there is no depth there. Instead of feeling the sheer joy of tearing through the depths of water, you end up in the mud at the base of shallow waters. Humiliated and soiled, he sits alone in a corner, alienated and feeling more vulnerable than ever before. You know what the fault was. The fault was not that he tried to network, but the fact that he tried to network outside of his own class. To fit in a totally different class, he makes compromises with himself, loses touch with his own class and keeps on going down the spiral, feeding on self-deprecation. Finally, he unmasks. He comes out as a lion in a club of wolves, who detest him for his majestic walk and come together to attack him. It is very important to find the right kind of people in your network, those who are like-minded and who share your mental space.

It is improbable that you do not know such people. Like-minded people know each other. It is very important to ensure that you land up in a group where people understand you, do not want you to be anything that you are not (as we argued earlier, all men are not equal, at least, not identical), allow you to build on your own merits without forcing you to contradict your own basic nature. The good part is that you are no longer pretending, nor are you sending forwarded messages on every occasion. Instead you are pausing every now and then, to look deep within. You start to dig out feelings of mutual respect, love and admiration while sending out messages to one another. When you speak well of the other, it is not because you want to feel good about lifting up a wretched soul with the crutches of lies, forced by the need to be socially correct, but rather you do so out of sheer truthfulness. Your praise is for the deserving ones and not for the bees that will return your kindness with poisonous stings. When you offer praise for the people who deserve it, you feel like you are doing a service to your own soul. Your soul is always looking to find fullness in this world of half-measures that you do not need or want anything in return. The virtuous, the evolving, the creative men, do not think that they do not need your words of support and solidarity, as they stand alone. Just like you, they too need reinforcement. They also need the common people to reassure them that they do not stand alone. You fulfill their needs of companionship, a need that each one of you have, lest you fall for those who are not worthy of your attention. You need to hold on to one another and be the other person's John Galt in this world where independent, individual enterprise is booed.

I have seen that in this world, if you list the ten most influential people, they would be known to each other and would be widely acclaimed as able people. If those ten people are in touch with each other socially then they all will be successful in all worldly parameters. Here, I do not implore you to give up your sensibilities, nor do I tell you to be non-judgmental, rather, I tell you to be true to your own sensibilities. Be judgmental and strive to reach out only to those people who are of your own, in thought and in deeds and then, work hard to be there for them, in their happiest and their loneliest hours, so that neither you nor they, stray into the market place of human soul where nothing is sacred and nothing is valued. It is your responsibility to protect each other from the absurdity of the trivial.

The problem is a problem of people skills. You work hard and you work well. You know everyone in your area of work. You know those who are like you but you do not reach out to them because you feel you are all that you are because you never perceived any weakness in yourself. You think that reaching out will mean that you are recognizing your weakness, your Achilles heel. You all admire each other but don't reach out to each other and keep on humiliating yourselves by attempting to be a part of a human mass that is not equal to you in either intellect or effort. This is the reason why it is important to find companionship in one another. Seek pleasure in the growth of each other, recognizing that each has his own size and potential. This creates a secret sect, an evolved society which appreciates the different statures of different people and does not cut all of them to the lowest factors to achieve uniformity.

You keep fighting with what you have and keep on bleeding, hoping for death or victory. Usually, it is death that comes first. Reach out; I tell you, reach out so that this flame of human excellence is not subjugated. Till you find your long lost brethren, may you find peace within yourself without stooping to lower order beings equal to you, neither in intellect, nor in passion.

*****

Love and Virtue

"It is virtue which both creates and preserves friendship. On it depends harmony of interest, permanence and fidelity"

- Cicero

The moment we show some indication of an ability to comprehend and learn, we are taught to love all alike. Gradually, it becomes such a deep rooted necessity that the negation of your affectionate overtures at any point later in life, by anyone, leaves you feeling worthless and out of spirit.

You keep on shouting, as you are pushed down the abyss. You shout the names of people you love and more than that, you want to be loved by them. Your voice traverses the complete distance and comes back with your questions unanswered, with such a violent force that it shakes you up. You struggle to keep yourself grounded, through rejections and betrayals, trying to hide behind some faith or religion or some God. You assign your cause to those imaginary Gods and then seek solace in the assumption that since God wanted you to love all people, any failure is His failure and therefore, by implication, He is supposed to take care of you and help you handle the disappointments arising out of your endeavours to do what you have been told to do, for it has been prescribed by Him. You try to justify it by arguing that the pain and the sadness that you come across is uplifting, since it comes as an outcome of something that you, as part of a larger human race, were ordained to do.

The collective religious wisdom pushes us to believe that we are to forego self-interest, care for people who are not virtuous, (love one and love all, irrespective of whether or not they deserve to be loved or whether or not we are sufficient enough to love). On this basic premise, which I find fallacious, we seek out to people who are non-deserving and end up hurting ourselves, and even then, rather than correcting or questioning the philosophy that our religious and cultural upbringing has thrust upon us, we feel that we somehow got hurt in the process of trying to do something we are ordained to do by someone or something higher than us. Our wounds should be a medal of our commitment to a larger love and therefore, we ought to be respected for it. I feel, these wounds we gain in the process, are a sign of immaturity and stupidity and it is a way of nature asking us to correct our thought and vision and get better. We feel that we are destined to love everyone, without any wisdom or discretion and consider the pain in the event of failure, as a step towards evolution, which it is, provided you are ready to evolve into a philosophy different from the "Love All things."

Somewhere, you demand respect for the wreck that you turn yourself into, looking down at people who are not willing to follow the ordained path according to your understanding, and moving towards the closure of the great drama of life, unloved and somewhere, deep down, unhappy. Sometimes, the masses make idols of you. But what is the outcome of this tiresome exercise? What do you have to show in the end, which can give you enough courage to say at the end of it, when the curtain is coming down and the fat lady has sung "Was it life? Let us do it once more." Think about the sum total of your existence on Earth.

The problem is on account of the unwillingness to question the basic premise upon which you have built your whole life. You were told that God wanted you to love all people in equal measure, without differentiation. Who says that this is what God has said? Is it not a conspiracy of the people who wanted you to completely love them and no one but them that they tried to bring in the fear of God? If scriptures were to be believed and if God, if at all, said that, then could it be that He Himself was so insecure and wanting that he had to invent heaven and hell to ensure that he be loved by all men? How would the fear of hell that God and God's men try to scare us with be different from the street urchin, threatening us to throw acid bottles on the face of women that they want to be loved by? When God has created you so different from all the other people he has created, would he not want you to be loved and respected for the difference? You were created as a unique person and so were all other people, at least initially, before they finally decided to yield to the temptation of gaining security in numbers by becoming a lookalike, by becoming like any other people around them, by killing and strangulating their independent thought and finally joining the herd. You are not supposed to love equally; you are supposed to love uniquely. All people do not deserve your love; all those who do, do not deserve it in same amount and form. Some might not deserve your love at all. By wanting to love all, you push your mind to rationalize. Some argue that people who love or attempt to love indiscriminately do not stand true to reason. I'd rather say that they do try to reason just as any reasonable man would, with imagined reasons and convoluted logic.

Such people want their love to be returned in full or more than in full. This return, they think, could justify their love for someone who does not deserve love. "I know that they are not virtuous, but I still feel love for them because they love me." Sometimes when they give such reasons, they then hate the object for not loving them enough to satisfy the argument; "I know they are unworthy, but still love them because that is what God has ordained me to do." Sometimes when they give such reasons, deep inside hate God for it; "I know they are not virtuous but I still love them because, that is the way for me to justify my being." Sometimes they say this and then hate life and their own selves for it. I urge you to refute all these, and pledge to never hide behind these. One, loving someone does not automatically make it mandatory for someone to love you back, rather, give your love only to those whom you can love even if they do not return it. Second, do not love anyone for the fear of hell or for the greed of heaven; what is heaven anyway? Some place where you get anything and everything without working for it, without deserving it! Three, it is a pity that you should need to love the unworthy to justify your existence. Can you not do any better, create something, achieve something, and scale some heights, to justify your existence? All this would essentially leave us with a very clear choice for the object of our love, those we can love without lure or fear, and those we can love even when we are not sure of being loved in return, that is to say, love only the virtuous.

And what is Virtue? Virtue is the commitment to stay true to the spirit of humanity, the spirit which mandates learning and creativity as the sole guiding force. The man whose growth is not stalled, either because he feels himself to be so small that he is incapable of doing anything great or because he feels himself to be so big that there is nothing further to go. Truly lacking in virtue is not the man who is in the process of attempting to build something and not yet successful, but the one who has given up trying to create.

When I tell you that love must be given only to the virtuous, I take the sting out of love. There is nothing like unreturned love. When you love someone virtuous, you do not want your love to be returned. You simply love and stand to gain by an affectionate observation of the object of your love, through which you grow and gain. Sometimes as you practice virtue, you do get the love in return. But that is just coincidental. It may or may not happen. You must stay true to yourself. It is always more fun to stand erect and enjoy the happiness of watching a giant than to break the back and try to be friends with a dwarf.

By loving someone virtuous and deserving, you allow yourself to stretch out to your potential rather than crumbling and folding yourself into something which is so sub-you that you hate yourself for it. It is a love which is nourishing and it must not be rushed. There is no opportune moment for you to find that object of love; it is something which will happen only if it has to. No calculation and no design can delay or hasten it. You cannot rush love. You need not go wanting for it. It might not happen in this lifetime but if you take what I write to your heart, then you will keep trying your best to be true to your own virtue. Then, there will always be at least one candidate who will be worthy of your love, that is, you! Do not go around trying to fill the void created on account of your lack of love for your own self, by substituting it with a love for someone who is neither virtuous nor deserving. If you cannot find sweet music, enjoy the silence; any attempt to fill it up with loud cacophonies will only leave you hurt, betrayed and with a bad headache.

It is not necessary that you will find the person who is rightfully deserving of your love, right from the time you stretch your arms wide out, looking and searching. But do not lose heart. Do not compromise on the universal commitment that we have made to our own selves, from the moment we come to existence, to find that one person who gets better with every passing day and in turn, inspires us to do the same and in whose presence the mind is charged with a passion to look at every act we do or do not do and reject or accept the course of action, which takes us closer to reason. This discovery may happen today, tomorrow, the next month or in many years. The longing, the search, the journey will be as fulfilling as the final discovery of the right companion, as the manifestation of virtues and values which you hold so dear to your own self. The finding, the final act is the culmination of a lifelong preparation for the great moment, a preparation which involves a very lonely path, wherein many a times you are prompted to strike a compromise with life and to try to hasten love. It is so silly and confounding to try to stage manage something so out of the world as love is; to hasten love. As Khalil Gibran puts it, "Try not to guide the path of love, for love, if it finds you worthy enough will guide you". Our aim is not to manipulate the factors or to surrender to some make-believe love, derived out of necessity or physical desire, which at the end of the day, with objectives gained, leaves you sad and broken, with a feeling of having been short-changed. Our aim is to enhance our worth, by putting every act of ours to the test of reason, by abandoning all that does not stand to reason and by holding on tightly to what does. Nothing should be driven by need and necessity. Let all be driven by reason. Keep the space around you vacant for the virtuous love to be accommodated so that once it finds you, you may feel its warmth in your skin. Gain the virtue so that on a glorious day, when love crosses your path, it is amazed at what you have become through continuous evolution. Your inner peace will guide love to you, and finding you worthy, uncorrupted by the commonplace, love will take you under its wings and guide your flight. Till such a time arrives, love yourself, look inside, for nothing can substitute a love which is true. Just as a writer should not write a story till the story lifts your pen and forces you to write, similarly anything done otherwise, because you feel it is what is being done around you and therefore should be done ends up as a slime piracy and as bad grammar, with stale thoughts, leading to a story that cannot survive even one night.

*****

Facing Your Demons

"All you have to do is to look straight and see the road, and when you see it, don't sit looking at it- Walk"

- Ayn Rand

I write this piece, at the break of dawn. Actually, a few moments before that, as the night is breathing its last breaths and a day, pregnant with hopes is about to begin. A thought comes to my mind; it wakes me up from my slumber and throws the pen right into my hands. Face your demons, says a voice somewhere, and I start writing, trying to find the meaning of the words that had echoed in my mind in the silence of the night.

We live through life half asleep, without coming to terms with what we are capable of, fully or even anywhere near it. So many a stories keep moving in and out of our persona without being written. The large canvas that life has provided us largely remains unpainted. A beautiful symphony remains unsung.

We try to find solace in invented reasons, sheepishly calling our lack of courage our practicality. No, there is nothing practical about not doing what you were created to do, may be created not by any rhyme or reason, but out of the stroke of sheer luck. Does it not make it even dearer that something so great was bestowed in your shape, out of sheer luck?

And what have you done with all that you were born with? You stifled it out of breath by strangulating it so hard that sometimes even tears flow from the corner of your eye. Pushing it into a corner, you buried it deep inside. You buried it so deep that after a while, you forgot about it or at best, you remember it vaguely. Do you remember it as a small figure you make on the glass through the moist cloud on a winter morning? Do you feel it as a song that sometimes plays in the back of your consciousness as you sift through the meaningless chores around you?

Maybe what you chose to do is not meaningless at all, for it keeps you alive and breathing. Of course it is practical to do it. But if it is not part of your preparation for the moment when you can stand out in the glorious light in perfect posture, with grace and panache, then it is really meaningless. It is nothing but all that you keep on doing to stay breathing. You love every moment with that song pushed to the back of your mind, the poems shunned from your lips and the story exchanged for some factual reports you write. You push yourself to a state where you are not even aware of the sweet promise that you were born with, a promise that lurks somewhere deep inside your heart; you kill the promise that nature made to you when you were formed out of null, and with it you kill every bit of you within your person.

I urge you to face your demons, for time is little and fleeting. You spent your life collecting currency to buy something, the love of which you were born with and now you have fallen in love with the currency.

You took a path to take you to a destination and now that you have reached the destination, you refuse to embrace it with open arms, for you say, you love the path that you have traversed. Or are you scared of the responsibility that embracing your passion will put on you? Is it the fear of doing it? But are you not scared of the prospects of ending the act with a dead song on your lips? Is the fear of not doing what you are meant to do not bigger than of doing what you are meant to do?

Face your demons, I urge you, not only for the deepest promise that you were born with but for everything that you thought was a whim and everything that you piled on the back of the racks in your orderly and well arranged thoughts, whether it is going out wearing that old leather jacket, or getting wet in the rain. Are you worried that you will make a fool of yourself? It is better than being one and missing out on the precious moment of time, that will never come back. Are you worried of slipping and failing? By not attempting, you have failed already.

A request, a plea, a demand lies lazily on your lips and you cup your mouth with your hands so that no one may see it. You try to keep it hidden so that the delicate balance which you think life to be is not disturbed, the equilibrium not broken. Disruption is the key. Break the mould! Do what has never been done before. You are not happy with what you see around you, you sigh with pain, close your eyes and hope and pray for it to pass, to be able to open your eyes and see a changed reality. But why would and should anything change, when the ingredients that you are adding to the water heating up on fire in front of you are not changing? Why would the drink be different? You take a sip and hope it tastes different from how it tasted yesterday or the day before. Not finding it any different, you are thrown into pessimism and depression of melancholy. You forget that a predictable path is called so because it is meant to give a predictable result.

What is it that you are doing different from what you did yesterday. You are still afraid of stepping on your own pinky toes and of those around you. You are so addicted to the world around you and to the working of the world that all that you do and act is so stale that it smells of the dead. Step out in the Sun. Do what you have not done ever before or not in a long time. Sing a song, write a poem, kiss a forehead and if it makes you happy, a little dance is not too bad either.

Face your demons, spell out what troubles you and speak out from the rooftop. It causes embarrassment to you? Care not; happy and embarrassed is better than unhappy and unembarrassed. Having done it, you will find, it was not so bad at all. You might have felt that you have been taken for granted, but then, you have granted yourself to others and to life, at large. Make a noise, stand up and take back the right, the grant that you have given to others over your own life, for you have only one moment to do it. That moment is NOW. Every today is pregnant with the possibility of tomorrow, if you are ready to appreciate the urgency and to understand the fleeting nature of time. Earth does not move only in the event of earthquakes, it is moving at all times, rotating on its axis. But we fall only during earthquakes because at that time, we are not able to keep up with the pace of the surface below our feet.

Our lives stand on nimble toes, on the surface of time, and we will have to keep up with it, lest we fall on our face, for then there will be no getting up. Do not keep for tomorrow, for all we have is this moment. As you read, as I write these lines, as you sit thinking of what I have written, it is all about this moment. The universe has been in existence for endless eons and will be there, global warming notwithstanding. The longest of lives are not even a flicker, on the large arms of the enormous clock hands that move on the gigantic walls. All that we have is now and today. Later will be too late; Promise yourself not one more moment of dead dreams, not one more moment of borrowed life. Have courage, seek out, be blatant and bold, for failure will be of minor value and success will be all that you were brought to existence for. Can anything be more wonderful than facing your demons and can anything be scarier than not facing them? Call up someone you have not called but have wanted to. Now! Write that book you always wanted to write. Now! Take a vacation. Now! Take your kid for a walk. Now! Stand up for what you think is right. Now! Every moment is a challenge thrown at us by life and I will not come short of it at any cost. The glory of success and of making an attempt will always outweigh the staleness of passivity and inactivity. Do what is right, what stands true to either one of the two tests, reason or passion, and do it with complete responsibility, as you do it for your own self. This, you owe to yourself. As Shaw puts it, "Just do what must be done. This may not be happiness but this is greatness."

*****

About the Author

Born in Pathankot in 1971, the author grew up at various places. Being the only son to an IAF personnel, he spent his formative years in Kanpur, Jalpaiguri, Patna and Guna in MP, before moving on to gain an engineering degree from Raipur and Masters in International Business from Indore. Through a very normal childhood, and very average and predictable educational journey for an Indian middle-class boy, a trace of eccentricity pushed him into writing poetry, while toggling along with the intricacies of telecom networks. Charmed by the idiosyncrasy of relationships, held so dearly and complexities of life and created such anxieties which can only be addressed by literally, spreading them out in the front and then trying to analyze the underlying designs; These essays are one of those attempts to explore and understand those designs.

He can be reached at ssuryesh@gmail.com

Serene Woods

Serene Woods (http://www.serenewoods.com) is an online portal launched to encourage emerging authors and photographers to showcase and sell their work.

'Words' – our world of books is an online portal where an emerging author, whether he is a five year old or a fifty year old, can launch himself. In simple words, if you have an original piece of writing, you can come on to the portal and put your book up for sale with sample excerpts for people to preview before buying. Readers, looking for new authors, can simply come on to the site and order their copy and the book is delivered at their doorstep.

'Memoirs' – our world of photographs is an online portal where emerging photographers can showcase their photographs and sell them as a piece of art or a collector's item.

For further details, you can contact us at contact@serenewoods.com

www.ingramcontent.com/pod-product-compliance
Lightning Source LLC
Chambersburg PA
CBHW060657030426
42337CB00017B/2656